NEO-HUMANIST STATEMENT OF SECULAR PRINCIPLES AND VALUES

NEO-HUMANIST STATEMENT OF SECULAR PRINCIPLES AND VALUES

PERSONAL, PROGRESSIVE, AND PLANETARY

Paul Kurtz

Institute for Science and Human Values

Prometheus Books

59 John Glenn Drive
Amherst, New York 14228–2119

Published 2011 by Prometheus Books

Inquiries should be addressed to
Prometheus Books
59 John Glenn Drive
Amherst, New York 14228–2119
VOICE: 716–691–0133
FAX: 716–691–0137
WWW.PROMETHEUSBOOKS.COM

15 14 13 12 11   5 4 3 2 1

Library of Congress Cataloging-in-Publication Data

Kurtz, Paul, 1925–
    Neo-humanist statement of secular principles and values : personal, progressive, and planetary / by Paul Kurtz.
        p. cm.
    ISBN 978–1–61614–354–1 (pbk. : alk. paper)
    1. Secular humanism. I. Title.

BL2747.6.K877 2011
144—dc22

                                                                      2010029631

Printed in the United States of America on acid-free paper

CONTENTS

Preamble   7

1. The Next Step Forward   11

2. Secular Humanism   15

3. Science and Skepticism   17

4. Human Values   21

5. Personal Morality/Good Will   25

6. Progressive Humanism   29

7. Planetary Humanism   31

8. Political Action   35

9. New Transnational Institutions   39

10. Historical Antecedents   45

Signers   55

PREAMBLE

Humanism has been transforming the modern world. We introduced the term "Neo-Humanism" to present a daring new approach for dealing with common problems. Neo-Humanist ideas and values express renewed confidence in the ability of human beings to solve the problems we encounter and to conquer uncharted frontiers.

For the first time in history our planetary community has the opportunity to peacefully and cooperatively resolve any differences that we may have. We use the term "community" because of the emergence of global consciousness and the widespread recognition of our interdependence. The worldwide Internet has made communication virtually instantaneous, so that whatever happens to anyone anywhere on the planet may affect everyone everywhere.

While most decisions that concern human beings are made by them on the local or national level, some issues may transcend these jurisdictions. These include emergency concerns such as regional wars and gross violations of human rights as well as more stable developments such as new ideas in science, ethics, and philosophy. Of special significance today is the fact that we inhabit a common planetary environment. In this context, activities in any one country may spill over to others, such as resource depletion and the pollution of the atmosphere and waterways. Of particular concern is the phenomenon of global warming, affecting everyone on the planet. Similarly, the possible outbreak of an epidemic or plague (such as the swine flu, tuberculosis, and wide-reaching malaria) can have global consequences. Here it is vital to coordinate activities for the distribution of vaccines, application of common quarantine policies, and so forth.

Increasingly, many other issues are of concern to the planetary community and may require cooperative action, such as the preservation of unique species and ecosystems, prevention of excessive fishing on the high seas, management of economic recessions, development of new technologies with their promise for humankind, amelioration of poverty and hunger, reduction of great disparities in wealth, seizing the opportunities to reduce illiteracy, addressing the need for capital investments or technical assistance in rural areas and depressed urban centers, and providing for public sanitation systems and fresh water. Of special concern is the need to liberate women from ancient repressive social systems and attitudes and to emancipate minorities, such as the untouchables in India, who suffer from religious prejudice and caste systems. Similarly, gays and other sexual minorities need to be liberated wherever they suffer harsh punishment because of their sexual orientations. The list of indignities is long indeed and a constant campaign for education and improvement is essential.

We submit that science and technology should be used for the service of humanity. We should be prepared to reconstruct human values and modify behavior in the light of these findings. In a rapidly changing world, fresh thinking is required to move civilization forward. We are concerned with reconstructing old habits and attitudes in order to make happiness and well-being available for every person interested in realizing the good life for self and others. Accordingly, this *Neo-Humanist Statement of Secular Principles and Values* is offered as a constructive contribution to the planetary community.

1

THE NEXT STEP FORWARD

There are various forms of religious belief in the world today. Many of these (though surely not all) stand in the way of human progress. This Neo-Humanist Statement aims to provide an agenda for those who are skeptical of the traditional forms of religious belief, yet maintain that there is a critical need to bring together the varieties of belief and unbelief and provide a positive outlook for the benefit of the planetary community.

Believers include all of the major religions (Christianity, Islam, Judaism, Hinduism, Confucianism, Taoism, Shinto, and some forms of Buddhism, etc.) and also the many denominations within each. It is estimated that there are 4200 religions or faith groups, ranging from dogmatic extremists who are certain that they are right to religious liberals who are receptive to new ideas and dialogue. Where creeds are deeply entrenched, rooted in faith and tradition, it may be difficult to reconcile differences.

Historically, believers have often attempted to suppress dissent and persecute heretics. The conflicts between Protestants and Roman Catholics, Sunni and Shiites, Hindus and Muslims, continuing to this day, have at times erupted into violence.

At the other end of the spectrum of unbelief stand the atheists, historically a small minority, who focused primarily on the lack of scientific evidence for belief in God and the harm often committed in the name of religion. The "New Atheists" have been very vocal, claiming that the public has not been sufficiently exposed to the case against God and his minions. We agree that the lack of criticism is often the rule rather than the exception. We point out, however, that the community of religious dissenters includes not only atheists, but secular and religious humanists, agnostics, skeptics, and even a significant number of religiously affiliated individuals. The latter may be only nominal members of their congregations and may infrequently attend church, temple, or mosque, primarily for social reasons or out of ethnic loyalty to the faiths of their forbearers, but they do not accept the traditional creed. *Ethnic identities can be very difficult to overcome*, and may linger long after belief in a given body of doctrine has faded—sometimes for many generations. Although such individuals may be skeptical about the creed, they may believe that without religion the moral order of society might collapse.

Religious identity has been instilled in children, at the earliest ages, so much so that it may define a person; as such it may be difficult to say that one is no longer an Irish Roman Catholic, Jewish, or a Greek Orthodox Christian—even though he or she may reject the religion per se and no longer believe in its creedal tenets. For religion not only entails a set of beliefs, but a way of life, a commitment to cultural traditions, and institutionalized moral practices and rituals. Critics of religion may only focus on its beliefs, which are taken literally, whereas many believers interpret them metaphorically or symbolically, and judge them functionally for the needs that they appear to satisfy.

Perhaps the strongest case against religions today is that they are often *irrelevant* to the genuine solution of the problems faced by individuals or societies. For the major religions are rooted in ancient premodern nomadic or agricultural cultures that, in many ways, render them no longer applicable to the urban, industrial, and technological planetary civilization that has emerged.

In our view of the current scene, not enough attention has been paid to Humanism as an alternative to religion. Humanism presents a set of principles and values that began during the Renaissance and came to fruition during the modern era. It marked a turning point from the medieval concern with the divine order and salvation to an emphasis on this life here and now, the quest for personal meaning and value, the good life and social justice in modern democracies and economies that served consumer tastes and satisfactions.

Humanists today sometimes differ as to its meaning. Some humanists have attempted to appropriate the term "religious," using it in a metaphorical sense. Among the self-described religious humanists, we may find people identified with liberal Protestant denominations, Unitarian Universalists, secular Jews, lapsed Catholics, Muslims, or Hindus, and even some who wish to distinguish the "religious" quality of experience from religion. Although they are naturalistic humanists rather than supernaturalists and do not believe in a transcendent God, they wish to encourage a new humanist cultural identity based primarily on ethical ideals that are humanistic.

2
SECULAR HUMANISM

On the other side of this debate stand the *secular humanists* who are wholly nonreligious and naturalistic. They do not consider their stance *religious* at all; they think this term obfuscates matters; so they differ with liberal religious humanists. They draw their inspirations primarily from modern sources: preeminently science but also philosophy, ethics, secular literature, and the arts. Moreover, many may even wish to join secular-humanist communities and centers in order to share bonds of human kinship and friendship. The term "Neo-Humanism" best describes this new posture, which aims to be more outgoing and receptive to cooperation with a broader network.

What then are the characteristics of Neo-Humanism as set forth in this Statement?

***First,* Neo-Humanists aspire to be more inclusive.** They will cooperate with both religious and nonreligious people to solve common problems. Neo-Humanists recognize that countless generations of human beings have been religious and that we often need to work together with religious people to solve common sociopolitical problems. But Neo-Humanists themselves are *not religious*, surely not in the literal acceptance of the creed. Nor do they generally adhere to a religious denomination, except nominally. They look to science and reason to solve human problems and they wish to draw upon human experience to test claims to knowledge and values. On the other hand, Neo-Humanists are *not* avowedly antireligious, although they may be critical of religious claims, especially those that are dogmatic or fundamentalist or impinge upon the freedom of others. They understand that neither emotion, intuition, authority, custom, nor subjectivity by itself can serve as a substitute for rational inquiry.

3

SCIENCE AND SKEPTICISM

Second, **Neo-Humanists are skeptical of traditional theism.** They may be agnostics, skeptics, atheists, or even dissenting members of a religious tradition. They
think that traditional concepts of God are contradictory and
unsubstantiated. They do not believe that the Bible, the Koran,
the Book of Mormon, or the Bhagavad Gita are divinely
revealed or have a special spiritual source. They are skeptical of
the ancient creeds in the light of modern scientific and philosophical critiques, especially, the scholarly examination of the
sources of the so-called sacred texts. They are critical of the
moral absolutes derived from these texts, viewing them as the
expressions of premodern civilizations. Nevertheless they recognize that some of their moral principles may be warranted,
and in any case deserve to be appreciated if we are to understand
their cultural heritages. They consider traditional religion's
focus on salvation as a weakening of efforts to improve this life,

here and now. They firmly defend the separation of religion and the state and consider freedom of conscience and the right of dissent vital. They deplore the subservience of women to men, the repression of sexuality, the defense of theocracy, and the denial of democratic human rights—often in the name of religion.

Neo-Humanists, however, are aware of the dangers of an overly zealous atheism such as emerged in Stalinist Soviet Union and Eastern Europe under totalitarian communism or Maoist China, where totalitarian atheists responded to the conservative Orthodox Church in Russia by closing churches, synagogues, and mosques and persecuting ministers of the cloth. Neo-Humanists believe in freedom of conscience, the right to worship or not, and they abhor any kind of repression whether at the hands of atheists in the name of the state or theological inquisitors in the name of the Bible or Koran.

Third, Neo-Humanists are best defined by what they are for, and not by what they are against. They aim to be *affirmative*. Although they are able and willing to critically examine religious claims that are questionable, their focus is on constructive contributions, not negative debunking. They are turned on by positive possibilities, not negative criticisms.

Fourth, Neo-Humanists use critical thinking to evaluate claims to knowledge by reference to evidence and reason. Claims to knowledge are most effectively confirmed by the methods of science where hypotheses are tested objectively. In those areas where scientific inquiry has not been effectively applied, every effort should be made to bring the best methods to bear so that beliefs are considered reliable if they are rationally justified. Thus claims to knowledge in principle are open to modification in the light of further inquiry, and no belief is beyond reexamination. The reflective mind is essential in evaluating the beliefs of people.

4

HUMAN VALUES

F ifth, Neo-Humanists apply similar considerations to the evaluation of ethical principles and values. These grow out of human experience and can be examined critically. They are most effectively judged by appraising their consequences in practice. Indeed, there is a body of ethical wisdom that has been developed in human civilization, though old moral recipes may need to be reevaluated and new moral prescriptions adopted.

Sixth, Neo-Humanists are committed to key ethical principles and values that are vital in the lives of human beings. These are not deduced from theological absolutes, but evolve in the light of modern inquiry. Among these are the following:

A key value is the realization of a life of *happiness and fulfillment* for each person. This is a basic criterion of humanistic ethics.

This does not mean that "anything goes." Individuals should seek the *fullest actualization* of their best interests and capacities taking into account the interests of others.

In the last analysis, however, it is *the individual person* who is the best judge of his or her chosen life stance, though there are a number of criteria that resonate with humanists, including the following:

The creative development of a person's *interests* should be balanced with one's preexistent *talents and values*.

The *rational life in harmony with emotion* is the most reliable source of satisfaction. This means that a person should be in cognitive touch with external reality, and his or her own innermost needs and wants—if the good life is to be attained.

A person should strive to achieve the highest standards *of quality and excellence* that one can.

Seventh, Neo-Humanists recognize that no individual can live isolated from others, but should share values with others in the community.

That is why *compassion* is an essential ingredient of the full life. This entails the capacity to love others and accept their love in return.

This involves some mode of *sexual fulfillment and compatibility*, the willingness to overcome excessive repression, given the diversity of sexual proclivities. Women's needs should be considered equal to men's, and society should tolerate same-sex modes of expression.

It also means that society should seek to cultivate *moral growth* in both children and adults.

No person is complete unless he or she can *empathize* with the needs of others and have a genuine *altruistic concern* for their good.

Such feelings are generated at first within the *family*, where children are made to feel wanted and loved.

Children need to develop in time a sense of *responsibility* for their own well-being, but also for the well-being of others within the family and also for their friends and colleagues, and indeed for all persons within the community at large, and beyond to all of humankind.

Eighth, Neo-Humanists support the right to privacy as a central tenet in a democratic society. Individuals should be granted the right to make their own decisions and actualize their own values, so long as they do not impinge on the rights of others.

Ninth, Neo-Humanists support the democratic way of life and defend it against all enemies domestic or foreign. *The civic virtues of democracy* have taken a long time to develop, but are now well established; they provide for the principles of *tolerance, fairness,* the *negotiation of differences,* and the *willingness to compromise.*

PERSONAL MORALITY/ GOOD WILL

*T*enth, **Neo-Humanists recognize the fundamental importance of good character in both personal life and the impact of a person on society.** Historically, many nonbelievers, secularists, atheists, and agnostics have de-emphasized the topic of personal morality, for they were turned off by the language of sin, and the calls for repression by the virtue police. They preferred to deal with questions of social reform. But it is clear that this is a mistake and that it is foolhardy not to deal with the question of good character and the moral integrity of the individuals who make up society. We need to develop enlightened individuals who have achieved some measure of ethical maturity and moral virtue.

Accordingly, the moral education of children and young persons is of special concern to parents

and society. This consideration also applies to adults, who may be married, have a job working with others, or participate in community affairs. Thus some guidelines would be useful, not enforced by legislation—unless a person harms others—but as parameters for evaluating behavior. Actually, there is wide consensus on many of these, and it is shared by members of the community. It cuts across religious or nonreligious lines.

We wish to point out that to be a secularist is no guarantee of virtue and that many evil acts have been committed by both religious and nonreligious persons. Hence the relevance of the Humanist outlook can be evaluated in an important sense by whether it provides personal meaning and moral purpose for the individual.

Unfortunately, people sometimes are nasty, uncaring, and insensitive to other people's needs. They have been overwhelmed by hatred, jealousy, greed, or lust— whether they are religious or not. The quest for power is often an inducement for corruption.

We submit that a good will to others is a basic moral principle that expresses a positive attitude toward life. How does this spell out in practice? A person of good will is kind, honest, thoughtful, helpful, beneficent, generous, caring, sympathetic, forgiving, fair-minded, and responsible. These are the *common moral decencies* that are essential for a peaceful and just society.

The authoritarian personality, on the contrary, is often avaricious, suspicious, power-hungry, prejudiced, cunning, cruel, ruthless, mean-spirited, selfish, demeaning, resentful, inflexible, or vindictive.

The person of good will needs to combine reason and compassion, the reflective mind and the caring heart. Therefore Neo-Humanism clearly has a list of desired and commendable personality traits by which we may evaluate the conduct of others: these are normative values and principles tested in civilizations by their authenticity. Those who violate the principles of decent behavior may be judged by the consequences of their conduct.

PROGRESSIVE HUMANISM

*E**leventh**,* **Neo-Humanists accept responsibility for the well-being of the societies in which they live.** Neo-Humanists support *the rule of law,* but also the application of the principles of *equality before the law* and *social justice.*

This includes equal treatment of all persons in society no matter what their social status—class, ethnicity, gender, or racial, national, or religious background. Neo-Humanists support *Progressive Humanism;* that is, the view that it is the obligation of society to guarantee, as far as it can, equal *opportunity* to all persons. These include the *right to education, universal health care,* the right, wherever possible, to be *gainfully employed* and to receive *adequate income* in order to lead lives in which their *basic needs may be satisfied.*

Neo-Humanists generally support a *market economy* as the most productive mode for achieving and expanding the economic wealth of societies, one that optimizes entrepreneurial talent with a just distribution of economic benefits.

They support a *fair taxation* system, and a *welfare concern* for those who, due to some incapacity, are unable to support themselves. This includes a social concern for people with disabilities, and a *just retirement system for the aged.*

Neo-Humanists eschew utopian schemes. Along with a commitment to the principles of Progressive Humanism, there is a commitment to realism; for they recognize that progress is often slow and painful, achieved piecemeal. Nonetheless they are committed to the *melioristic* view that through persistent courage and intelligent action it is possible to create a better world. Accordingly, we are committed to the above set of noble goals.

PLANETARY HUMANISM

*T*welfth, **Neo-Humanists support a green economy wherever feasible.** A growing concern today is *environmental degradation and pollution.* In the quest for new sources of clean energy, every person should consider her or himself as a guardian of nature and should help to limit over-fishing of the seas, protect whenever possible the extinction of other species, and stop the pollution of the atmosphere. The planet Earth should be viewed as our common abode; each person has an obligation to preserve the environment, at least in his or her own domain. The callous destruction of rainforests and the acidification of river estuaries should be a concern to every person on the planet. Neo-Humanists advise humans to cultivate *affection* for this blue-green planet, Mother Earth, and a devotion to its renewal.

Among the highest virtues that we can cultivate is some *reverence for nature*, and an appreciation of the bounty that it affords for the human and other species.

It no longer is the right of anyone and everyone to plunder the richness of nature and to denude its resources.

We have an obligation to future generations yet unborn, and a moral responsibility to *ecohumanism*; namely, a loving care and concern for our planet and life on it.

Thirteenth, Neo-Humanists recognize the urgent need for some form of population restraint. This includes guaranteeing women the right to autonomy in matters of pregnancy.

We deplore the opposition, based on theological doctrine, of some powerful religious institutions to block effective policies to limit population growth. It is estimated that there were 200 million humans on the planet in the year 1; 310 million in the year 1000; 1.6 billion in 1900; 2.5 billion in 1950, and over 6 billion in the year 2000. If present trends continue, the Earth is projected to soar to 7.5 billion by 2020 and to over 9 billion by 2050. There is thus an urgent imperative to reduce the rate of population growth. With the improvement of medical science, public health, and sanitation, fortunately there has been a continuing decline in the death rate; but this means a surging population. In the past, humanists had always been in the forefront of those advocating rational population policies. These have been rejected by reactionary religious forces who have opposed voluntary contraception and/or abortion. That the green revolution will continue to provide abundant harvests is problematic. There is no guarantee that droughts will not devastate crops. Hence, the runaway growth of population is a gnawing problem that humankind needs to deal with forthrightly.

Related to this is the fact that the percentage of older persons in many societies is increasing. People over sixty now number one in ten in the developed world. This is expected to increase to two in nine by 2050. Whether the working population will be able to support those who are retired will become a critical issue in the future. The upshot of this is the need to constantly revise public policies in the light of altered social conditions. It is clear that economic-moral principles are crucial in guiding public policies in the light of changing economic realities.

8
POLITICAL ACTION

Fourteenth, **Neo-Humanists recognize the need to participate actively in politics.** Although humanist organizations generally have not endorsed candidates or political parties, a compelling argument can now be made that they should organize politically. The Christian Coalition and the Roman Catholic Church, Muslim, Hindu, and other religious denominations do so in democratic societies; why not secular humanists? We know that many humanists are active politically as individuals in political organizations; however, they have not as yet organized collectively with grassroots politics to meet challenges from the Religious Right and other politically organized groups, as well as to advance humanist social views.

One reason why they have resisted taking political positions is because of the nonprofit status in many countries of their organizations, which are precluded from doing so. This does not prevent Neo-Humanists quite independently organizing or joining political pressure groups, or entering into coalitions with other groups in society with whom they agree, or applying for a different tax status for a new affiliated organization that could engage in politics.

Another reason why they have eschewed taking political positions is that there has been a tendency to define secular humanism by its opposition to religion and many secular humanists have thought that as long as a person was an atheist or agnostic they shared a basic principle with others. Thus many right-wing libertarians were attracted to the antireligious stance of the secular humanists, though they rejected what they considered to be its too liberal economic agenda, which was labeled as "left wing."

We submit that the terms "left wing" or "right wing" are holdovers from earlier periods in history and have little meaning on the current scene. Very few object to the role of the Federal Reserve in the United States or similar government bodies in other countries from initiating programs of economic stimuli to jump-start faltering economies or to rescue financial institutions from bankruptcy. Nor is there any objection to supporting a strong defense budget, scientific research, space research, or institutes of health or education. Ideological symbols may generate rhetoric, but they do little to deal with concrete problems faced by nations.

Yet one can argue that the ethics of humanism is merely a set of abstract generalizations until it has some application to social problems. Relating Neo-Humanism to concrete issues of concern to society may very well attract a significant portion of the unaffiliated and discontented people in our society who may be looking to become involved with a Humanistic outlook that makes sense to them. Indeed, we can and do appraise economic policies in the light of humanist values and this has political implications. One of the purposes of humanism is to evaluate political and social organizations by their ability to *enhance* human life. Neo-Humanist organizations accordingly must be prepared to engage in political action.

Fifteenth, Neo-Humanists need to take progressive positions on economic issues. We offer the following moral guidelines:

The overemphasis on price and profit in the past as the primary criteria of merit has led many to focus on "cash value." Many are wont to herald people of wealth as the paragons of social worth. This overlooks scientists, Nobel Prize winners, teachers, political leaders, artists, poets, or dedicated members of the helping professions, and the fact that many social activities are performed by nonprofit institutions or that government has a role to perform in society.

There are several ethical principles that constrain the free market as the primary arbiter of social utility. One is expressed by Immanuel Kant's *second categorical imperative*, namely, *that we should treat persons as ends not as means*. This, according to Kant, is based upon reason, and it provides essential constraints on certain forms of economic behavior.

There are other *imperatives* that place limits on unfettered free markets. We are referring here to a growing list of *human rights* that have developed in democratic societies. For example, we affirm our respect: for the right to life, liberty, and the pursuit of happiness, yes— but without discrimination rooted in gender, sexual orientation, race, ethnicity, or creed; the right to education of every child, and other rights as enumerated above.

Progressive tax policies are essential in a just society. These policies have been adopted by virtually every democratic society on order to provide a level playing field so that equality of opportunity is made available to all individuals. In addition there are many social needs that cannot be fully implemented by the private sector alone and need the public sector: the common defense, roads and waterways, public health, science, and education, to mention only a few.

Extreme disparities in income and wealth are characteristics of unjust societies, and progressive taxation is the fairest way to prevent these.

A progressive humanist is aware of the powerful contributions that free markets make to the prosperity of nations. But the principles of social justice should also be part of our moral concern and the fruits of a free society should be made available to as many members of society as possible. Although the gross domestic product is an important criterion of economic progress, we also should seek to elevate the *gross national quality of life*. We should encourage people to achieve lives of satisfaction, excellence, and dignity; and to persuade them by means of education to develop their aesthetic, intellectual, and moral values, and thus enhance their quality of living.

9

NEW TRANSNATIONAL INSTITUTIONS

S *ixteenth,* **Neo-Humanists recognize that humanity needs to move beyond egocentric individualism or the perspective of chauvinistic nationalism. The planetary community needs to develop new transnational institutions.** The new reality of the twenty-first century is the fact that no one on the planet can live in isolation, and every part of the world community is interdependent. This applies equally to nation-states, which are arbitrary jurisdictions based on historic contingent events of the past. The failure of the 192 nations meeting in Copenhagen in December 2009 to reach an accord that effectively controls global warming points to the urgent need to establish new international institutions.

There is a need for a new transnational agency to monitor the violation of widely accepted environmental standards, to censure those nations that do, and to enforce such rules by the imposition of sanctions.

The challenge facing humankind is to recognize the basic ethical principle of planetary civilization—that *every person on the planet has equal dignity and value as a person,* and this transcends the limits of national, ethnic, religious, racial, or linguistic boundaries or identities.

We reiterate the ethical obligation of all members of the planetary community to transcend the arbitrary political boundaries of the past and help create new transnational institutions that are democratic in governance and will respect and defend human rights.

To solve global conflicts, new transnational institutions need to maintain the peace and security of the citizens of the world and guard against violence and force. Eventually humankind will need an adequate multinational force subordinated to the established world authority to maintain peace and security. The United Nations peacekeepers serve as a model that needs to be strengthened.

Transnational institutions will need to adopt a body of laws which will apply worldwide, a legislature to enact and revise these laws, a world court to interpret them, and an elected executive body to apply them.

These institutions will allow a maximum of decentralized local and regional governance. They will foster the growth of multisecular societies in which individuals will be encouraged to participate in the democratic processes of governance and maximize voluntary choice. The cultural traditions of various areas will be respected, although an appreciation of the commonly shared ethical values of all peoples will be encouraged.

Transnational institutions will deal with questions that overlap jurisdictions. They will encourage world commerce and trade, and will work with the governments of the world to maximize employment, education, and health care for the populations of the world.

They will attempt to deal with environmental threats, such as global warming, and the pollution of the atmosphere and waterways, and to safeguard endangered species.

They will seek to rid the world of disease and hunger, and endeavor to overcome the vast disparities in income and wealth.

They will encourage cultural enrichment and an appreciation for the sciences and the arts.

They will seek to facilitate the growth and availability of universal education for all age groups without discrimination. They will defend the rights of the child: Every child needs to have adequate nourishment and shelter; every child has a right to knowledge of the arts and the sciences and the history of the diverse cultures of the world.

The transnational institutions will encourage open media, the free exchange of ideas and values. They will try to enrich human experience by encouraging travel, leisure, and recreation.

The purpose of these transnational institutions is to extend humanistic values and enable the good life to be experienced by all members of the human family. We now possess the scientific technology and know-how to bring this about. For the first time in human history, we can rise above the national, ethnic, racial, religious, and cultural barriers of the past. The ethics of planetary humanism make it clear that every person on the planet is precious and that we need to develop empathetic relationships and extend outreach and good will everywhere.

If humanity is to succeed in this noteworthy endeavor it will need to marshal confidence that at long last we can achieve the blessings of liberty, peace, prosperity, harmony, and creative enjoyment for all, not only for my national, ethnic, racial, or religious group, but for everyone. What a noble idea to strive for: the happiness of humanity as a whole, and for every person in the planetary community.

These are the vital principles and values that a secular, personal, progressive, and planetary humanism proposes for humanity. It is a Neo-Humanist Statement for our time.

Heretofore the great battles for emancipation, liberty, and equality were on the scale of nation-states. Today the campaign for equal rights and for a better life for everyone knows no boundaries. This is a common goal for the people of the world, worthy of our highest aspirations. Given the emergence of electronic media and the Internet, people can communicate across frontiers and barriers. Thus we are all citizens of a planetary village, where new ideas and values can spread instantaneously. If we set our minds to it, there is no reason why we cannot achieve these glorious ideals. We should resolve to work together to realize an ancient dream of the solidarity of human beings. We now are fully aware that we share a common abode, the planet Earth, and that the civilizations that have evolved have a responsibility to overcome any differences and to strive mightily to realize the ideal of a true planetary community.

We who endorse this Neo-Humanist Statement accept its main principles and values. We may not necessarily agree with every provision of it. We submit that the world needs to engage in continuing constructive dialogue emphasizing our common values. We invite other men and women representing different points of view to join with us in bringing about a better world in the new planetary civilization that is now emerging.

This statement was drafted by Paul Kurtz.

* * *

10

HISTORICAL ANTECEDENTS

The above Neo-Humanist Statement of 2010 is the sixth such document. Five major humanist manifestos and declarations have previously been issued in the twentieth century.[1] These documents are endorsed by several hundred humanist leaders of thought and action worldwide. They have been translated into a great number of languages. The first five spanned the years from 1933 to 2000. They were issued to meet the special challenges and problems of their day. Nonetheless there are common principles and values that appear in all of them. As such, perhaps they may constitute a "humanist canon," or at the very least a framework of the meaning of humanism.

Humanist Manifesto I was published in 1933. It was endorsed primarily by Unitarians, who sought to defend liberal religious humanism. The term "religious" was used by the American philosopher John Dewey, who also signed *Manifesto I*.

Dewey said that one could develop a set of inspiring naturalistic ideals and values that motivated us to action, yet was not a supernaturalistic religion. *Manifesto I* stated that *Manifesto I* was written at the height of the Great Depression of the 1930s. As such, it stated that "religious humanists regard the universe as self-existing and not created . . ." for human beings are "part of nature." "Modern science makes unacceptable any supernatural or cosmic guarantee of human values." Religious humanists affirmed that "humanism considers the complete realization of human personality to be the end of man's life." These sentiments were shared by other humanists who did not wish to consider themselves "religious." Many humanists, such as Sidney Hook and Corliss Lamont, objected to "God language." However metaphorical, they opted for nonreligious humanism. *Manifesto I* was written at the height of the Great Depression of the 1930s. As such, it stated that "the existing acquisitive and profit-motivated society" was inadequate, and that "a socialized and cooperative economic order must be established." This provision did not survive in subsequent Manifestos and Declarations, which allowed for a variety of economic systems—libertarian, social democratic, or mixed.

Humanist Manifesto II (1973) appeared after World War II during the Cold War between Western democratic societies and Marxist-Leninist-Maoist countries, which were engaged in dangerous ideological controversies. Meanwhile the United Nations was founded after the war and many avowed humanists played a leadership role in its early days.[2]

What was unique about *Manifesto II* was its recognition that a new moral revolution was under way in many societies. It forthrightly defended human rights such as contraception, abortion, sexual freedom between consenting adults, divorce, and euthanasia—all opposed by conservative religionists. This *Manifesto* defended the rights of women and minorities and urged tolerance for alternative sexual preferences and lifestyles. It did not take a stand between religious and nonreligious forms of humanism, recognizing that religion played a significant role in America and other societies. The *Manifesto* was very critical, however, of dogmatic and authoritarian religions and it expressed skepticism about immortal salvation or eternal damnation. Distinctively, *Humanist Manifesto II* affirmed a new humanistic ethics, not based on theology but human experience. It emphasized the importance of reason and science in solving human problems.

This *Manifesto* affirmed the rights of the individual person as a central humanist value. It defended civil liberties, participatory democracy, and the separation of church and state. It deplored the division of humankind on nationalistic grounds, urged the world community to renounce the resort to violence and to engage in cooperative planning concerning the use of the Earth's rapidly depleting resources and excessive population growth. It stated that the problems of the global economy cannot be solved by one nation alone, for they are global in scope. It also responded to the Luddites of the day by stating that the growth of technology is "a vital key to human progress." In response to repressive totalitarian societies such as the Soviet Union, it recommended that we must "expand communication across frontiers." It closed with the recommendation that humanity needs to be able to rise above competing economic and political systems that divide the world. "Each person," it said, "should become a citizen of the world community."

Humanist *Manifesto II* was initially endorsed by hundreds of humanist leaders of thought and action worldwide. It received wide coverage by the international media, including a front-page story in the *New York Times*, and stories in *Le Monde*, the *London Times*, and *Pravda*.

We did not realize that it would provoke such strong protests from many conservative religionists, perhaps due to a failure on their part to appreciate its constructive contributions. Most humanists today consider *Humanist Manifesto II* to best crystallize their outlook. In retrospect, *Humanist Manifesto II* was also critical of Islam, which began to emerge from its dogmatic slumbers. Indeed, it responded to fundamentalisms of all sorts—whether Christian, Islamic, Judaic, Hindu, or other.

The protests against secular humanism intensified in the United States in the late 1970s and '80s, for its critics maintained that secular humanism had inordinate influence on the intellectuals, the media, the universities, the courts, politics, and liberal institutions. Unfortunately, no one came forth at that time to defend, let alone define, secular humanism. This led to the publication of a *Secular Humanist Declaration* in 1980. This document was again endorsed by leading public intellectuals and scientists.

The *Declaration* began by stating that "secular humanism is a vital force in the contemporary world. It is now under unwarranted and intemperate attack." It deplored the fact that the world is faced by a variety of "anti-secularist trends." This *Declaration* sought to defend democratic secular humanism by emphasizing certain key principles. "The first principle of democratic secular humanism is its commitment to free inquiry." It pointed out that civil liberties were vital for democracies, which totalitarian communist countries did not respect. It highlighted the importance not only of the separation of church and state, but official ideology and state as well. The ideal of freedom was the underlying value that was vital for modern democratic societies.

This *Declaration* again emphasized the centrality of humanistic ethics, based on critical intelligence, not ecclesiastical or theological assumptions. It objected to the efforts by any one church or religious sect to impose its moral principles on the greater society. It emphasized the value of human happiness here and now, not ancient revelations of salvation. It maintained that human beings can "lead meaningful and wholesome lives for themselves and in service to their fellow human beings . . . without religious commandments or the benefit of clergy." It recommended "that secular education should be cultivated in children and young adults."

An essential point that needs to be reiterated is that the *Secular Humanist Declaration* did not espouse atheism per se. It stated clearly that "secular humanists are skeptical about supernatural claims," but it also added that "we appreciate the fact that religious experience often gives meaning to the lives of human beings," though it denied that this is rooted in the supernatural. A key principle of the *Secular Humanist Declaration* that is highly controversial today in the light of "the new atheists" is its statement: "Secular humanists may be agnostics, atheists, rationalists, or skeptics;" though they deny "the claim that some divine purpose exists for the universe," secular humanism is thus not synonymous with atheism.

The *Declaration* goes on to deplore "the attacks by nonsecularists on reason and science." At the time when the *Declaration* was published, creationism was being widely touted and "the theory of evolution was under heavy attack by religious fundamentalists." Evolution is so basic to modern science that to deny it is to ignore the abundant evidence that supports it. The

Declaration urged that education should be the essential method of building humane democratic societies, and that secular humanists need to "embark upon a long-term program of public education and enlightenment concerning the relevance of the secular outlook to the human condition." "We affirm," it declared, "that we can bring about a more humane world . . . based upon the methods of reason, tolerance, compromise, and the negotiation of differences." It concluded that we deplore "the growth of intolerant sectarian creeds that foster hatred."

Reading this *Declaration* retrospectively today, it is clear that *secular humanism does* not *require atheism as a necessary precondition*. Secularism implies three key ideas: (1) It is clearly non-religious; (2) It maintains that human values *are rooted* in human *experience and critical intelligence*. This entails an emphasis on *this life here and now*, not salvation or punishment in the next life; and (3) the term "secular" also refers to the *separation* of church and state. Although secular humanism is not equivalent to atheism or agnosticism, it is nonetheless highly skeptical of supernatural claims; and encourages biblical and koranic scholarly and scientific criticism.

A new challenge has emerged today to confront secular humanism; for several secular authors have advocated "the new atheism." These include Richard Dawkins, Christopher Hitchens, Daniel Dennett, Sam Harris, and Victor Stenger. They insist that there is sufficient evidence for atheism and urge that secular humanists aggressively advocate the view that "God does not exist," that the classical religions are false, that people who believe in them are deceived, and that their ethical values are also false. The new atheists have published several books that have become mini-bestsellers. They have received widespread public attention, and this has attracted some secular humanists who insist that *secular* does imply atheism (or agnosticism). For a variety of reasons, we submit that this position is mistaken, for it has distorted both secular humanism and humanism in general. We reaffirm that secular humanists are (a) skeptical of supernatural claims, (b) do not think that there is sufficient evidence for God's existence, and (c) do not believe the historical claims of revelation in the Bible or the Koran are evidential. (d) Ethics should be independent of theological foundations; nor do we think (e) that we should lampoon or ridicule religious believers per se. (f) We should indeed critically examine the many claims of religious traditions with a skeptical eye, and (g) and we should be willing to engage in constructive dialogue and debate with those within the religious communities. (h) Although we may profoundly disagree with our religious colleagues and/or adversaries, we should be tolerant, respectful, and dignified. (i) Even though we may disagree about fundamental doctrinal, philosophical, or theological issues, our discourse should be civilized.

With this in mind, we have proposed a new form of humanism that is not antireligious per se, nor avowedly atheist. We submit that there is an urgent need for a new humanism in the world today; hence *Neo-Humanism*. This form of humanism has two vital components in its philosophical outlook. The *first* emphasizes the need to cultivate an appreciation for science and reason. In concrete terms this has meant developing "critical thinking" and using "the method of intelligence" or "the methods of science"; namely, all hypotheses, theories, or beliefs should be tested, validated, confirmed, or justified by reference to evidence and reasons that support the claims. The *second* vital component of Neo-Humanism is the conviction that ethical values are related to human experience; they are amenable to critical evaluation and may be modified in the light of such inquiry.

It is especially important that humanists appeal to a wider base of support. Some 16 percent of the American population is not affiliated with any church, temple, or mosque—approximately 50 million Americans—whereas only 2 to 3 percent are estimated to be out-and-out atheists. Hence, Neo-Humanism wishes to address its message to a broader public who we believe should be sympathetic.

The new atheists surely have played an important role in contemporary society, for they have been willing to question the foundations of theism, a topic often considered *verboten* until now. One should not overlook the fact that the old atheism had a strong impact in the nineteenth and twentieth centuries, insofar as it was allied with Marxism, including its totalitarian versions. Indeed, the communists at first attempted to eradicate religious institutions from the societies in which they ruled, and this led to extensive persecution of believers.

There are varieties of unbelief, and one can be skeptical of religious claims, or be virtually indifferent to religious creeds, yet seek a fulfilling moral life and contribute to the social good. It is too narrow to identify humanism with atheism or even agnosticism, for one can reject the lure of religious salvation on other grounds. *The main point of Neo-Humanism is its recommendation that we adopt a positive humanist agenda.* This is the position of the scientific naturalist who begins with nature and life, as viewed from the perspective of reason and science, without the baggage of ancient religions. Contemporary civilization has progressed beyond that.

We need to reaffirm the viability and appeal of *humanism* for the future of humankind. This was clearly stated in *Humanist Manifesto 2000*:

> Humanism is an ethical, scientific, and philosophical outlook that has changed the world. Its heritage traces back to the philosophers and poets of ancient Greece and Rome, Confucian China, and the Carvaka movement in classical India. Humanist artists, writers, scientists, and thinkers have been shaping the modern era for over half a millennium. Indeed, humanism and modernism have often seemed synonymous; for humanist ideas and values express a renewed confidence in the power of human beings to solve their own problems and conquer uncharted frontiers.
>
> Modern humanism came to fruition during the Renaissance. It led to the development of modern science. During the Enlightenment it germinated new ideals of social justice and inspired the democratic revolutions of our time. Humanism has helped frame a new ethical outlook emphasizing the values of freedom and happiness and the virtues of universal human rights.
>
> [We] believe that humanism has much to offer humanity. . . . Many of the old ideas and traditions that humankind has inherited are no longer relevant to current realities and future opportunities. We need fresh thinking if we are to cope with the [planetary] society that is now emerging. . . .

Accordingly, we have presented a Neo-Humanist Statement that we submit incorporates the best aspects of the humanist outlook: it is secular, personal, progressive, and planetary in outlook. Its aim is to invite dialogue and discussion with all sectors of public opinion in order to advance the cause of humanity.

NOTES

1. (1) *Humanist Manifesto I* (1933); (2) Humanist *Manifesto II* (1973); (3) *Secular Humanist Declaration* (1980); (4) *A Declaration of Interdependence: A New Global Ethics* (1988); and (5) *Humanist Manifesto 2000* (2000)

2. These include Sir Julian Huxley, first head of UNESCO, Lord Boyd Orr, head of the World Food Organization, and Brock Chisholm, head of the World Health Organization.

Signers

A Neo-Humanist Statement of Secular Principles and Values has been endorsed by the following individuals (*institutions are for identification only*).

UNITED STATES

Norm Allen, former executive director, African Americans for Humanism

Philip Appleman, poet and Distinguished Professor Emeritus, Indiana University

Louis Appignani, entrepreneur and philanthropist

Khoren Arisian, PhD, senior leader emeritus, New York Society for Ethical Culture

Joe Barnhart, professor emeritus of philosophy and religion studies, University of North Texas

Baruj Benacerraf, PhD, Nobel laureate in physiology or
     medicine
Paul D. Boyer, Nobel laureate in chemisty
Gwen Brewer, professor emeritus, California State University,
     Northridge
Margaret Brown, PhD, social scientist
Arthur J. Caplan, professor, University of Pennsylvania
Robert D. Carl, CEO and chairman, Health Images, Inc.
Carleton Coon, former diplomat and ambassador
Nathan Curland, technologist
Elizabeth Daerr, environmental business owner
Edd Doerr, president of Americans for Religious Liberty and
     past president of the American Humanist Association
Michael Dowd, former pastor, science educator, author
Ann Druyan, writer/producer, CEO Cosmos Studios
Arthur Engval, superconduction engineer
Edward L. Ericson, former senior leader, New York Society for
     Ethical Culture, past president, American Ethical Union
Valerie Fehrenback, PhD, clinical psychologist
Owen Flanagan, James B. Duke Professor of Philosophy, Duke
     University
Stanley Friedland, PhD, educator and author
Hugh Giblin, activist and author
Rebecca Newberger Goldstein, philosopher and novelist,
     Harvard University
Robert Goodrich, president/owner, Goodrich Quality
     Theaters, Reality Radio WPRR
Sheldon F. Gottlieb, biologist/physiologist, University of
     South Alabama
D. J. Grothe, president, James Randi Educational Foundation
Adolf Grünbaum, Andrew Mellon Professor of Philosophy of
     Science, University of Pittsburgh

Thomas Harrison, retired bank officer

Herbert A. Hauptman, Nobel laureate in chemistry

Larry A. Hickman, director, Center for Dewey Studies, professor of philosophy, Southern Illinois University, Carbondale

R. Joseph Hoffmann, professor of religion, Goddard College

Samuel Ilangovan, MD, director, Periyar International, USA

Stuart D. Jordan, PhD, NASA, Goddard Space Flight Center

Philip Kitcher, John Dewey Professor of Philosophy, Columbia University

William Knaus, PhD, psychologist, Albert Ellis Institute

David R. Koepsell, JD, PhD, attorney, philosopher, University of Technology, Delft, The Netherlands

Lawrence M. Krauss, theoretical physicist

Jonathan Kurtz, president, Prometheus Books

Paul Kurtz, professor emeritus of philosophy, State University of New York at Buffalo

Gerald A. Larue, professor emeritus, University of Southern California

Colin McGinn, professor of philosophy and Cooper Fellow, University of Miami

Dale McGowan, PhD, executive director, Foundation Beyond Belief

Rachel Alina Michaels, Columbia College, Chicago

William R. Murry, Unitarian minister, past president and dean of Meadville Lombard Theological School

Joe Nickell, PhD, author, senior research fellow, Committee for Skeptical Inquiry

Terry O'Neill, president, National Organization for Women (NOW)

Vincent Parr, PhD, clinical psychologist, Albert Ellis Institute

Steven Pinker, Harvard College Professor and Johnstone
     Family Professor of Psychology, Harvard University
Anthony B. Pinn, professor, Rice University
Howard Radest, former head, Ethical Culture Schools
James Randi, founder, James Randi Educational Foundation
Peter Rogatz, MD, physician-executive
Patricia Schroeder, former member of the U.S. House of
     Representatives
Elliott Sober, Hans Reichenbach Professor of Philosophy,
     University of Wisconsin
Jerome Stone, professor emeritus, William Rainey Harper
     College
John Sutter, president, Democratic World Federalists
Robert B. Tapp, professor emeritus, University of Minnesota
Carol Tavris, PhD, social psychologist
Lionel Tiger, professor of anthropology, Rutgers University
Toni Van Pelt, public policy activist
Carol Wintermute, co-dean, The Humanist Institute

ADDITIONAL SIGNERS

David A. Bennett, rationalist
Bob Carroll, professor of philosophy, Sacramento City College
J. Beth Ciesielski, educator, director of Bridges for
     Education, Inc.
Ronald Defenbaugh, pharmacy owner
Jefferson T. Dorsey, attorney specializing in capital defense,
     federal and state public defender (retired)
Jan Eisler, nurse practitioner
Stephen Ervin, professor emeritus of zoology, California State
     University, Fresno

Bert Gasenbeek, University for Humanistics, Utrecht,
    The Netherlands
Paul Heffron, PhD, professional musician
Steve Horn, director of public library
Philip E. Johnson, PhD, retired teacher
Dwight Gilbert Jones, humanist philosopher
Katherine S. Kaiser, retired social worker
Thomas J. Moore III, information technology, program/project
    manager
Vir Narain, air marshal, Indian Air Force (retired), Indian
    Humanist Union
Fredrick Rea O'Keefe, CEO, Advanced Industrial
    Technologies
Chad M. Pawlenty, industrial plant manager
Bill Reitter, president, American Humanists for Peace
Richard Glenn Rich, commercial estimator, freethinker, deist,
    Decatur, Alabama
David Rush, MD, professor emeritus of nutrition, community
    health, & pediatrics, Tufts University
Melissa Sandefur, social scientist
David Schafer, president, HUUmanists Association (Unitarian
    Universalist Humanists)
Erich Vieth, founder, Dangerous Intersection
Cookie Washburn, landscaping professional
Eric Adair Whitney, USCG (retired)

INTERNATIONAL

Mona Abousenna, professor emeritus of English, Ain Shams
    University, Egypt
Mario Mendez Acosta, science writer, Mexico City, Mexico

Pieter V. Admiraal, MD, PhD, retired anesthesiologist,
    The Netherlands
Floris van den Berg, philosopher, Utrecht University, The
    Netherlands
Bill Cooke, former president, Association of Rationalists and
    Humanists, New Zealand
Christopher diCarlo, associate academic professor of
    philosophy of science and ethics, University of Ontario
    Institute of Technology, Canada
Captain Paul Drouin, MM MNI, Lac-Beauport, Quebec,
    Canada
Stephanie Louise Fisher, PhD student, Nottingham
    University, United Kingdom
Christopher C. French, professor, Goldsmiths, University of
    London, United Kingdom
Jan J. Hodes, teacher of history, optician, Zutphen,
    The Netherlands
Leo Igwe, founder, Nigerian Humanist Movement
Valerii Kuvakin, professor of philosophy, Moscow State
    University
Stephen Law, senior lecturer in philosophy, Heythrop College,
    University of London, United Kingdom
Gerd Lüdemann, professor of history and literature of early
    Christianity, University of Gottingen, Germany
Radmila Nakarada, professor and director of peace studies,
    Faculty of Political Science, Belgrade, Serbia
Innaiah Narisetti, author and journalist, professor, Hydrabad
    University, India
Manuel A. Paz-y-Mino, president, International Institute of
    Applied Philosophy, Peru
Jean-Claude Pecker, astronomy, professor, College de France

Amanda W. Peet, associate professor of physics, University of
Toronto, Canada

Alexander Razin, professor of philosophy, University of
Moscow, Russia

Barbara Stanosz, retired professor of philosophy, Warsaw
University, Poland

*Svetozar Stojanovic, professor, University of Belgrade, Serbia

Rodrigue Tremblay, PhD, emeritus professor, University of
Montreal

Mourad Wahba, founder, Afro-Asian Philosophy Association,
Egypt

*deceased

(Other names are being added)

If you agree with the main principles of the Neo-
Humanist Statement, please add your name and your pro-
fession or institution. (Institutions are for identification
only.)

Please email your agreement to: paulkurtz@aol.com.